I0893554

SLOTHS ARE AWESOME

by Samantha S. Bell

12 STORY LIBRARY

www.12StoryLibrary.com

12-Story Library is an imprint of Bookstaves and Press Room Editions

Produced for 12-Story Library by Red Line Editorial

Photographs ©: Seaphotoart/Shutterstock Images, cover, 1, 4, 9, 14; Nacho Such/Shutterstock Images, 5; kungverylucky/Shutterstock Images, 6, 8, 29; worldswildlifewonders/Shutterstock Images, 7, 17, 23, 28; Adam King/Shutterstock Images, 10; Luiz C. Ribeiro/Shutterstock Images, 11; Martijn Smeets/Shutterstock Images, 12; Pavel Hlystov/Shutterstock Images, 13; Leonardo Mercon/Shutterstock Images, 15; Przemyslaw Skibinski/Shutterstock Images, 16; Kristel Segeren/Shutterstock Images, 18, 24; Janossy Gergely/Shutterstock Images, 19; nattanan726/Shutterstock Images, 20; Christopher Robin Smith Photography/Shutterstock Images, 21; Matthew W Keefe/Shutterstock Images, 22; Kevin Wells Photography/Shutterstock Images, 25; cvloet/Shutterstock Images, 26; anekoho/Shutterstock Images, 27

Library of Congress Cataloging-in-Publication Data
Names: Bell, Samantha, author.
Title: Sloths are awesome / by Samantha S. Bell.
Description: Mankato, MN : 12 Story Library, [2017] | Series: Animals are awesome | Audience: Grades 4 to 6. | Includes bibliographical references and index.
Identifiers: LCCN 2016047146 (print) | LCCN 2017004853 (ebook) (print) | LCCN 2017004853 (ebook) | ISBN 9781632354396 (hardcover : alk. paper) | ISBN 9781632355072 (pbk. : alk. paper) | ISBN 9781621435594 (hosted e-book)
Subjects: LCSH: Sloths--Miscellanea--Juvenile literature. | Children's questions and answers.
Classification: LCC QL737.E2 B45 2017 (print) | LCC QL737.E2 (ebook) | DDC 599.3/13--dc23
LC record available at https://lccn.loc.gov/2016047146

Table of Contents

1 Sloths Spend a Lot of Time in Trees

The tropical rain forests in Central and South America are home to many unusual animals. Sloths are no exception. These slow-moving creatures can be found eating and resting high in the trees. Sloths spend almost all of their time hanging upside down from tree branches.

Sloths often look as though they are smiling.

This makes it easy for them to hold on to tree branches while hanging upside down.

There are six species of sloths. All sloths have long, curved claws. They have three claws on their back feet. But their front feet have a different number of claws depending on the species. Linnaeus's two-toed sloth and Hoffmann's two-toed sloth have two front claws. The brown-throated sloth, maned sloth, pale-throated sloth, and pygmy three-toed sloth all have three front claws.

Except for when a mother sloth has a baby, sloths live alone. Sometimes more than one sloth will sleep in the same tree. But they do not do things together. When a sloth is ready to move to a new tree, it does not climb down. Instead, it uses large vines called lianas to cross from one tree to another.

3.5

Average length, in inches (8.9 cm), of a two-toed sloth's claws.

- Sloths live in rain forests in Central and South America.
- Sloths spend most of their time in trees.
- Sloths hang on to trees with their long front claws.
- Sloths use vines to move from tree to tree.

Sloths have long legs and a round head.

2

Sloths Have Special Fur

A sloth's fur is suited for hanging upside down. When a sloth is right-side up, its hair parts in the middle of its belly and grows toward its back. Even the hair on the sloth's face points upward. When the sloth is upside down, its hair looks as though it is facing the right way. If it rains, the water will run right off the hairs.

It is easy to tell three-toed sloths apart from two-toed sloths, even if you cannot see their claws. Three-toed sloths have short tails. They have dark masks around their eyes. Adult males have a large patch of short, golden-orange fur with a dark brown stripe down the middle of their backs. Two-toed sloths do not have a tail, a mask, or a fur patch.

Three-toed sloths are a little smaller than two-toed sloths. Three-toed sloths grow to be approximately 23 inches (58 cm) long

A Hoffmann's two-toed sloth hangs from a tree.

A young three-toed sloth sits in a tree in Costa Rica.

and weigh approximately 9 pounds (4.1 kg). Two-toed sloths can grow to 29 inches (74 cm) long and weigh up to 20 pounds (9.1 kg). But three-toed sloths have an advantage that two-toed sloths do not. They have extra vertebrae in their necks. This allows them to turn their heads 270 degrees around.

10

Maximum number of vertebrae in a three-toed sloth's neck.

- A sloth's hair parts in the middle of its belly and grows toward its tail.
- Three-toed sloths have a mask and a short tail.
- Three-toed sloths have extra vertebrae that allow them to turn their heads farther around.

THOMAS JEFFERSON'S GROUND SLOTH

President Thomas Jefferson's friends knew he liked to study fossils. Colonel John Stuart gave Jefferson a fossil that came from what is now West Virginia. At first, Jefferson thought the bones were from a giant, lionlike cat. After further study, he decided they were from a large extinct ground sloth. In 1822, the animal was officially named after him, *Megalonyx jeffersonii*.

3

Sloths Take a Long Time to Eat

Three-toed sloths eat only leaves. Two-toed sloths also eat flowers, buds, and shoots. Sloths eat from the tops of many different trees. Individual sloths have a few favorite tree species found within a small area. They will eat from these types of trees again and again.

Sloths chew their food for a long time before they swallow it. The cellulose in the leaves can be hard to digest.

Sloths hang upside down even when they eat.

DRASTIC CHANGES

One reason it takes a sloth so long to digest its food is because of changes in its body temperature. People have a regular body temperature of 98.6 degrees Fahrenheit (37°C). A sloth's body temperature can range from 82 to 104 degrees Fahrenheit (28–40°C). When the sloth's temperature drops, the chemical processes in its stomach slow down.

Some of the leaves are protected by toxic chemicals. But a sloth's slow digestive system helps it get rid of any poisons.

As much as two-thirds of a sloth's weight comes from the food in its stomach. Some food takes a month to go through the sloth's stomach. A sloth's large stomach helps with digesting food. The stomach has four separate chambers. They are good for storing the bulky food. Bacteria in the chambers help break down the food.

18

Number of teeth a pygmy three-toed sloth has.

- Three-toed sloths eat only leaves.
- Two-toed sloths eat leaves, fruits, flowers, and buds.
- Each individual sloth has its favorite kind of leaves.
- Sloths chew their food for a long time.
- Sloths have a four-part stomach with bacteria that slowly digests leaves.

Sloths have a limited diet.

4

Sloths Are the World's Slowest Animals

Sloths move so slowly that they seem lazy. They can climb only approximately six to eight feet (1.8–2.4 m) per minute. But they are slow for a few good reasons.

Sloths eat food that is easy to find, but it is not very nutritious. Leaves do not give sloths much energy. So they conserve their energy by being inactive. But sloths have another good reason for being slow. They do not have much muscle. Their muscles are smaller and weaker compared with other animals that are the same size. Most other mammals are 50 percent muscle mass, but sloths are only 25 percent muscle.

Three-toed sloths spend approximately only 10 percent of their time moving.

Being slow has its advantages. Because their metabolisms are so slow, sloths are able to survive some big injuries. When they are hurt or bitten by other animals, their wounds rarely become infected. Many times, sloths heal completely in less than a month.

THINK ABOUT IT

If people are injured, they may rest for a day, a week, or even several weeks. Ask a teacher, parent, or librarian to help you find out more information about how sleep affects healing. How does it compare with what you know about sloths?

41

Number of yards (37 m) a sloth may travel in a day.

- The sloth's leafy diet does not provide much energy.
- A sloth's body is only 25 percent muscle.
- A sloth's slow metabolism helps it heal quickly.

5 Sloths Are Great Swimmers

Sloths may be awkward on land, but they move well in the water. Sloths are really good swimmers. Sometimes a sloth drops from a tree into a river. Then it does the breaststroke with its long arms to swim across the water. When a sloth wants to move to a different location, it will often wait for the forest to flood. Then it can swim to a new place.

When sloths are not eating or swimming, they spend their time sleeping. Two-toed sloths are nocturnal. They sleep during the day and are active at night. On the other hand, three-toed sloths are both nocturnal and diurnal. Sloths sleep for 15 to 20 hours each day. They often curl up in a ball in the fork of a tree.

Sloths move easily through the water.

Sloths often curl up in a ball when they sleep. They look like a clump of leaves hanging in the trees.

Sometimes sloths sleep in the tangles of lianas that hang from trees. The vines provide good hiding places. They also alert the sloths to danger. A predator must shake the vines to get to a sloth, warning the sloth that danger is near.

INTERNATIONAL SLOTH DAY

The AIUNAU Foundation is a group dedicated to protecting all forms of wildlife. To help people learn about sloths, the foundation created International Sloth Day in 2010. The holiday is still celebrated each year in October. Some people celebrate by sleeping or relaxing.

6

Number of hours a sloth may spend eating each day.

- Two-toed sloths are nocturnal, while three-toed sloths are nocturnal and diurnal.
- Sloths swim using their long front arms.
- Sloths sleep most of the day.
- Sloths like to sleep curled up in a ball in the fork of a tree.

6 Sloths Grow Algae on Their Fur

Several types of predators are a threat to sloths. A jaguar will climb a tree to catch a sloth. Because a sloth does not weigh much, it can climb out of reach on the thin branches. But the sloth is still in danger. Harpy eagles might fly in and try to grab it. When the sloth sees a predator coming, it will move a little more quickly. But doing so uses up a large amount of energy.

The best defense a sloth has is to hide. Its fur helps it stay

Sloths can use their claws to protect themselves from predators.

Sloths blend in with their environment.

camouflaged. Sloth hair is long and coarse with grooves in it. The grooves collect rainwater. Algae grows inside the grooves. The algae makes the fur appear green, helping sloths hide among the leaves.

980

Number of beetles once found living in the fur of a single sloth.

- Harpy eagles and jaguars attack sloths in trees.
- Algae grows on sloths' fur.
- The algae helps camouflage the sloths from predators.
- Many different organisms live in a sloth's fur.

Three-toed sloths usually have more algae on their fur than two-toed sloths have.

A sloth's fur is just the right habitat for other organisms. Moths and beetles spend time in the fur of both two-toed and three-toed sloths. Mites and ticks live there, too. Some of these organisms cannot be found anywhere else on Earth.

THINK ABOUT IT

Some scientists call sloths "walking ecosystems." Look up the definition of an ecosystem. Do you agree or disagree? Why?

7

Sloths Poop Once a Week

With such a slow digestive system, sloths do not need to get rid of waste very often. Approximately once a week, a sloth will climb down a tree to poop. Three-toed sloths use their short tails to dig a small hole. After they are finished, they cover it up with leaves.

The ground is a dangerous place for a sloth to be. While on the ground, the sloth's back legs are not much use. They are too weak to support the sloth. The sloth must dig its front claws into the ground and pull itself along. Predators, such as a jaguar or ocelot, are a threat. Sloths will try to defend themselves by clawing and biting at their predators.

Scientists are not sure why sloths make the risky trip to the ground.

Sloths rarely come down from trees.

5

Number of feet (1.5 m) per minute a sloth can move on the ground.

- Sloths move on the ground by dragging their bodies.
- Sloths must watch out for predators, such as jaguars and ocelots.
- The only way sloths can defend themselves is by clawing and biting.

MOTHS, LARVAE, AND SLOTH POOP

Some scientists believe sloth waste helps moths that live in the sloth's fur. When the sloth climbs down the tree, the moths fly out and lay their eggs in the poop. The larvae eat the waste, create cocoons, and turn into moths. Then they fly into the trees to live in the fur of a sloth. The moths fertilize the algae in the sloth's fur, and more algae grows. Others think sloth poop helps fertilize the trees.

The trip is unsafe, and it uses up a lot of energy. Some people think it is a way for a sloth to spread its scent to other sloths.

Sloths drag themselves along the ground using their claws.

8

Sloths See in Black and White

Sloths have very poor vision. Their eyes are missing a tiny muscle that changes the lens in the eye. This keeps sloths from being able to focus on objects at different distances. Their eyes are also missing the cells that allow them to see in color. Sloths see only in black

Sloths do not see very well.

Sloths have very small ears and do not hear well.

and white, and they see best in dim light. Their pupils are usually small, even at night. They often blink only one eye at a time.

Sloths do not have good hearing, either. Their ears are small and covered in fur. They are tuned only to low-frequency, or deep, sounds. Sloths must rely on their senses of taste, touch, and smell instead.

Sloths do not have sharp teeth. They must use their hard lips to bite the leaves off trees. A sloth's tongue is long and thick. It has many tiny spines that point backward. The spines help move food to the back of the mouth so the sloth can swallow it.

0.5

Length, in inches (1.3 cm), of a brown-throated sloth's ear.

- Sloths have poor eyesight.
- Sloths see best in dim light.
- Sloths cannot hear well.
- Sloths have long, thick tongues.

9

Sloths Can Be Noisy

Sloths make a variety of sounds. If they are distressed, they may make a hissing sound. They might also make a low moaning sound, a grunt, or a bleat. Sometimes, three-toed sloths make a long, high-pitched call. It sounds as if the sloths are saying "ahh-eee." Some people call three-toed sloths "ais" because of the sound they make.

Female sloths are ready to find a mate when they are approximately

Sloths live alone, except for when they mate.

4

Age when a male sloth may begin looking for a mate.

- Three-toed sloths sometimes make loud calls.
- Female sloths scream to find a mate.
- If more than one male reaches a female at the same time, the males fight.
- Males fight while hanging by their feet from tree branches.

A three-toed sloth hangs from a tree.

three years old. To find a male, the female lets out a loud scream. The scream tells the males where to find her. When a female screams, more than one male might come at the same time. If that happens, the males will fight for the female. Sometimes, the males make a sound like a high-pitched whistle. Then they hang from the tree branches by their back legs, swing their arms, and paw at each other.

10

Sloths Give Birth in Trees

Sloths give birth while hanging upside down. Females have just one baby at a time. The newborn sloth already has fur and claws. It must grab onto its mother to keep from falling to the ground below.

A baby sloth hangs in a tree.

The baby sloth finds its way to its mother's belly. The mother's body forms a sort of hammock where the baby can rest. The baby begins to nurse right away. After approximately 10 days, the baby sloth tries eating solid food. It eats

12

Weight, in ounces (340 g), of a newborn two-toed sloth.

- Sloths have only one baby at a time.
- Sloths give birth while hanging upside down.
- The baby must grab onto its mother and start nursing.

leaves that have been chewed by its mother. But the baby continues to drink its mother's milk until it is approximately six weeks old.

The baby hangs on tightly to its mother. Hooking itself into her fur, it stays hidden. If the baby gets separated from its mother, it will cry out for her. This loud bleat usually lasts 30 to 90 seconds.

A baby sloth grabs onto its mother's fur and climbs onto her chest as soon as it is born.

11

Mother Sloths Carry Their Babies on Their Stomachs

The baby sloth first hangs upside down when it is approximately 20 to 25 days old. But it will continue to ride on its mother until it is approximately six to nine months old. It spends this time learning from its mother. She teaches it where to find shelter and what to eat.

Sloths can start hanging in trees on their own when they are only a few weeks old.

Some sloths may stay with their mothers for several years.

The leaves in the rain forest can be toxic. The mother sloth shows her baby where to find the best trees in her territory. She teaches the baby which leaves are safe. The baby keeps at least one foot on its mother as it reaches to eat the leaves. The baby eats whatever its mother eats. Her favorite trees become the baby's favorites, too.

3

Minimum number of weeks a baby sloth must wait before it can hang upside down.

- A baby sloth rides on its mother for six to nine months.
- Sloths may stay by their mothers for six months to two years.
- The mother sloth teaches its baby what to eat.
- A baby will live in the same home range as its mother.

Depending on the species, the baby will stay with its mother for up to two years. Eventually, the mother sloth will move on to another part of her home range. The young sloth will live on its own. It will use part of the home range its mother used. The mother and baby may even continue to call to each other.

12

Sloths Cannot Shiver

Predators are not the only things that can harm a sloth. Cold weather can cause major problems for these animals. Even in a tropical forest, sloths can get cold. Since sloths do not have much muscle, they cannot shiver to warm up. They must warm up in the sun instead. But if the weather is cool and rainy, a nursing female sloth could die.

When a nursing sloth is cold, the bacteria in her stomach cannot digest food. This is very dangerous for the sloth. If her baby is feeding, it will use up any nutrients in the

SLOTH RESCUES IN COSTA RICA

Many sloths live in Costa Rica. There are several sloth rescue organizations in this country. Rescue groups help orphaned and injured sloths. People set up sanctuaries where the sloths can recover. Then they release the sloths back into nature. People can visit or volunteer at the sanctuaries.

Sloths live only in places where the weather is warm most of the year, such as Panama.

Some people wrongfully think sloths are related to monkeys.

mother's body. The mother may starve and die. Then the baby might fall to the ground.

Cold weather is just one threat sloths face. Humans also pose a threat. Sometimes, sloths get hit by cars. Other times, they get caught in electrical wires. People hunt sloths or sell them as pets. Cutting down the trees in a rain forest makes it hard for sloths to find places to live. Trees protect sloths from predators and provide food for them to eat. Understanding sloths and their habitats is the first step in helping them survive.

20

Percentage of the Amazon rain forest that has been cut down in the past 40 years.

- Sloths do not have enough muscle to shiver when they are cold.
- If a nursing female gets too cold, she might die.
- The sloth's greatest threat is humans.
- People can help sloths by protecting trees in the rain forests.

THINK ABOUT IT

Some threats to sloths are natural. Others are human-made. With the help of a parent or teacher, look online for things you can do to help sloths.

Fact Sheet

- Sloths are related to anteaters and armadillos. Each of these species are unusual animals.
- Sloths are folivores, or leaf eaters. They get almost all of their water from the plants they eat.
- A sloth can rotate its feet almost 180 degrees. This allows it to reach tree branches.
- The scientific name for sloth is *Bradypus*. It is the Greek word for "slow feet."
- Some animals use scent to mark their territory. Male sloths leave their scents on tree branches.
- Female sloths are pregnant for 5 to 10 months. A two-toed sloth measures approximately 10 inches (25 cm) long when it is born.

- Sloths live approximately 12 to 20 years in the wild. They live approximately 30 years in captivity.
- Three-toed sloths do not do well in captivity. This is because of their restricted diet.

Glossary

bacteria
Single-celled organisms that live in soil, water, plants, and animals.

camouflaged
Having a protective coloration that helps animals blend in with their environments.

cellulose
The main substance found in plants.

chambers
Spaces or compartments.

diurnal
Active during the day.

lens
The clear part of the eye.

metabolism
The chemical processes that happen within the body to process food.

nurse
To drink a mother's milk.

nutritious
Something that provides nutrients for energy and growth.

ocelot
A medium-sized wildcat with a gray coat and black spots.

organisms
Living things.

predators
Animals that live by hunting, killing, and eating other animals.

toxic
Poisonous.

vertebrae
The bones and cartilage that make up the spinal column.

For More Information

Books

Arlon, Penelope, and Tory Gordon-Harris. *Scholastic Discover More: Rainforest*. New York: Scholastic, 2013.

Clark, Willow. *Three-Toed Sloths*. New York: PowerKids Press, 2012.

Gregory, Josh. *Sloths*. New York: Children's Press, 2016.

Index

About the Author

Samantha S. Bell lives with her family and lots of pets in the foothills of South Carolina. She loves writing about nature, and she is the author or illustrator of more than 60 books for children.